AFFIRMATIONS AND ANTIDOTES

THAT HEAL ME

SBG Media Group
ATLANTA

AFFIRMATIONS AND ANTIDOTES THAT HEAL ME

Copyright © 2017 by Marilyn E. Porter
All rights reserved. This book or any portion thereof
may not be reproduced or used in any manner whatsoever
without the express written permission of the publisher
except for the use of brief quotations in a book review.

Unless otherwise stated, all scripture verses are taken from
The King James Version of the Holy Bible.

ISBN: 97- 80999183724
Library of Congress Control Number: 2017954524

Printed in the United States of America

SBG MEDIA GROUP

www.thescatterbrainedgenius.com/publishing

CONTENTS

A Prelude to Healing	Dr. Marilyn E. Porter
Randie Forne	Until You Forgive Yourself
Rebecca Adams	Affirmations and Antidotes
Balkaran Singh	You Are Healing
Tiesha Frontis	Affirmations and Antidotes
Jessica Schuurman	Puzzle Piece
Twylia Reid	I am Victory
Jessica Schuurman	Affirmations and Antidotes
Twylia Reid	Affirmations and Antidotes
Annie Echevarria De Saquic	Healing Through ME
Tiesha Frontis	Affirmations and Antidotes
Joy Jallah	The Healing Process
Genae Kulah	Affirmations and Antidotes
Christina Wilson	Timing that Heals
Betty Speaks	Affirmations and Antidotes
Joy Jallah	God Can Restore Lives
Brittany Peterson	Affirmations and Antidotes

Healing unites us.

A Prelude to Healing

There is always a beginning that carries us to the end, healing is no different – you must begin somewhere. I want offer you a huge piece if wisdom where healing is concerned, and I do mean HUGE.
The word forgiveness has become a nasty little road block that gets in the way of grudges and paybacks (which by the way are rarely successful because as you are digging the grave for the other person, you often fall into yourself) – but forgiveness is a necessary ingredient to healing.

When we are hurt by anyone, in any way we tend to hand on to the why and how of the hurt that came upon – while not being aware of the hurts that we have caused others so the cycle of not forgiving stands in the way of the healing process for all.

I have but one desire in penning these words, and that is to request that you would allow healing to BE your choice from this moment forward. Choose to forgive them. Choose to forgive YOU. Choose to let it go because it can't be taken back, but it can hold you back from loving and growing and flourishing in this ONE life that we all have to live.
UNforgiveness is like preparing a drink of poison for the other person but instead you drink it yourself!
STOP DRINKING THE POISON!
Dr. Marilyn "M.E." Porter

Healing IS your birthright.

UNTIL YOU FORGIVE YOURSELF
Poet Randie Forne
Raleigh, NC

Momma said, "Son, I know you mean well, but try to understand.

I'm a single woman now and in love with a good man.

When you and he argue and don't see eye to eye,

my heart breaks into a million pieces and I just want to cry."

I said, "Momma, please listen while I explain.

He has a wife and three kids; there's nothing there to gain.

I don't mean to hurt you, Mom. It's not what I want to do.

I would put my life on the line and shed *blood* for the sake of you!"

Momma said, "I was a child when you were born; the day your father left.

And I did the best I could to raise you by myself.

Just because you're a full-grown man and you have left the nest—

Don't get it twisted son: Momma knows what's best.

So, don't you be confronting me."

I came home from work one night,

as the phone RANG off the wall.

Momma was hysterical when I received her call.

My mouth fell open in disbelief.

My body felt a shock!

By the wife of the man my momma loved, to death he had been shot.

I thought I heard the worst of it all,

But found out something else:

She shot and killed her own three children, then turned and shot herself.

Although it's been some years ago, Mom's not quite the same.

Although she strongly denies the guilt, she feels she is to blame.

She even takes sleeping pills but still wakes up at night.

She says that God is punishing her for not doing what was right.

"God has forgiven you, Mom", but my words don't seem to help.

"But, you'll never find the peace you seek,

Until you forgive yourself."

Rebecca Adams
Trowbridge, United Kingdom

Healing Affirmations

I am enough and I am worthy.

I am loved and divinely supported.

I am strong, confident, and full of gratitude.

Healing Virtue
Self-acceptance is the first step to the healing process.

You must remember that you are unique, blessed, and an incredible human being. Life is precious and I highly encourage you to find the blessing in each day in order to heal yourself from the inside out. Be patient and gentle with yourself—the healing process takes time.

I learned this firsthand through my divorce. At the time, I was experiencing a lot of negative emotions, which included anger, upset, and sadness from the betrayal. I had thoughts of, "How could he do this?" and "Why?" I started over-thinking and self-questioning myself constantly. My heart had been smashed into a thousand pieces, like when you drop glass on the floor, and I was so consumed with upset that I didn't know how to start the healing process as I was in the middle of the whirlwind of devastation. All I knew was that I couldn't go on feeling like I was, day in and day out, as I had myself and my two children to think about.

One afternoon everything changed for me. I had a knock at the door and it was a lady wanting payment from my soon-to-be ex-husband. I decided in that moment that *this*, right here, was not happening anymore: I could NOT be consumed by anger, upset, or stress. I told the lady I was not paying anything; she had to contact him herself. I stepped into my power and healing process.

No longer would I allow someone else to control my head through emotions. I needed to heal from the breakup of my marriage. I had to heal for myself and my children. I made a choice that it didn't serve me or anyone else for me to give in to the negative emotions. I needed to start the healing process straight away.

"Love is patient. Love is kind. It always protects, always trusts, always hopes and always perseveres. Love never fails" (1 Corinthians 13:4 and 13:7).

I am part of something bigger than myself (just like you are, too) and I knew that life happens "for" us to show us a different path along our journey so that we serve our bigger purpose. I let my actions define me and I poured so much love into my children, my vision, and goals that I had no more tears about the divorce process and the stress that tried to get me off-course along the way. I gained my own self-respect and respect from others as I didn't allow the negative emotions to pour out of me any longer. I showed loyalty to both myself and my children by keeping my eye on the target of self-healing and happiness.

In defining moments within your life, you have choices and they can change your perspective within your life, how you feel, what you do, and so on. YOU are in control of your reactions, so I encourage you to respond and not react to anything negative that comes your way—whether in life or business.

I focused on my own healing process, so I listened to music that made me smile. I took my children on days out to hear their laughter and see their smiles. I chose to focus on positive experiences and read books that helped me to stop over-thinking. This was part of my healing.

My main healing process was what I told myself and that was feelings of unworthiness and questions, so I chose to read my Bible and remember the scripture from Proverbs 31:10 *"She is worth far more than rubies"*. Lightbulb moment for me!

My mindset and healing changed from that point, so I started to repeat affirmations to myself daily in order to retrain my brain to really focus on what thoughts I was actually telling myself. I worked on me.

I healed from the anger, sadness, upset, betrayal, over-thinking, and self-questioning. I have realized that we are not here, on this beautiful planet, to be sad, angry, or upset. We are here to feel emotions of happiness, kindness, joy, and love.

The transition from a negative thought process to a positive one *can* be accomplished. You have to make the decision to start.

To have a new beginning, you need to accept yourself *as you are.* You need to be gentle with yourself, stay grounded, and remain balanced. You are here to help and heal others—and it all starts with YOU.

Be full of gratitude daily and gain clarity on your feelings. Know that you *can* heal and that it's part of your inner strength. Do it for yourself and your own heart, mind, body and soul.

Remember that you are enough, you are worthy, you are loved, and you are beautiful.

YOU ARE HEALING
Poet Balkaran Singh
Vancouver, British Columbia

There are no treasures
at the end of this—
no pots of gold.

There is only breathing.
That, is healing.

Only breathing of thinner air,
which won't carry
as much salt and water
as your eyes do now.

That, is healing.

There are no gods,
and you are not Achilles;
but your heels aren't dry
and there is salt spare,
for wounds salt them.

That, will be healing.

And what we excavate
from skin,
from muscle, and sinew—
from bone.

The trauma that has sat there
on its web and laid eggs
won't make us less human,
yet make us more god.

That, is healing.
To dry

open wounds in the day's scorch
and nurse them at night
in bandages
of salt
with pickled compresses
and look less for miracles
but know that
you are one.

That, will be healing.
That, will be our healing.
That will be salvation.

Because you are what you pray to.

You are the emblem.
You are scripture.
You are body of its word.
You are its prayer.
You are the guru.
You are earth.
She is your mother.
You are her child.
You are Nanak.
Gautam Christ.
Rahim Vishnu.
You are their flesh
and their light.

YOU ARE HEALING.

We aren't there yet, where self-scribed biographies can be filed.
We simply obsess over pens, and write.
~Balkaran

Tiesha Frontis
Durham, North Carolina

Healing Affirmation

I am Being Made Whole

Healing Virtue

I see myself as whole and I love me as I Am.
This reminds me that God is mending every broken piece in my heart, mind, and soul. I can rest assure that God loves me and His love will never fail. Through Him loving me, I have the strength to love me through my healing process.

Psalm 139:14 "I will give thanks to you because I have been so amazingly and miraculously made. Your works are miraculous, and my soul is fully aware of this."

Be thankful for who God created you to be. He made no mistakes when He created you. Loving you as you are will free your mind from negativity and believing the lies of the enemy. Continue to see yourself whole because you must begin to **believe** what you see in order for the manifestation to BE.

Healing Affirmation

I am wise.

Healing Virtue

I am mindful of my thoughts and wise in my words towards loving me. This reminds me I have power to change my circumstance with the words I speak and the thoughts I think.

Proverbs 19:8
"To acquire wisdom is to love oneself; people who cherish understanding will prosper."

There are times when we begin to tear ourselves down with our words and the thoughts we allow to enter our minds. In doing that, we begin to believe those negative thoughts about ourselves because of the things we have been through and life ups and downs. Learn to love yourself. Speak it daily and, in the process, you will acquire the wisdom from God to know what to speak over your life in order to change your situation, to heal your mind, to heal your heart, to heal your soul, and to prosper in your life.

PUZZLE PIECE
Poet Jessica Marie Schuurman
Edmonton, Alberta

My head lay flat under the clear water,
Listening to what is simply our overlapping heartbeats.
There is more to this life than what I have pondered;
Being filled with nothing but fear, allowing my heart to beat.

This curiousness of flattery, for where the boat roams;
I cannot take another minute to bear the thought of you grown.
In this world of plunder, I stand in search of HIS thunder.
For who knew HE'D be the one to save my soul?

Holding you for the first time, so familiar and past due.
So pure and innocent, my child; you have brought the light to view.
Quivering in the dark corner, the enemy knew his time was over.
The battle was lost, as a warrior was born to conquer.

We stand together united, holding the hands of the righteous.
I cry out in battle to save you from the darkness.
You healed me and all my emptiness, giving me
the vision that our father loves us.

Forever will I admit, you as my saving grace;
My son, my light, my angel.
Forever and eternity, I will stay true and on purpose
Alongside our almighty LORD AND SAVIOUR!

Twylia Reid
Savannah, Georgia

MY NAME IS VICTORY

I AM victorious!
I AM a winner!
I AM above and not beneath!
I AM the head and not the tail!
I AM worthy of all good things!
I AM the righteousness of God!
I AM strong in the Lord and in His mighty power!
I AM an overcomer!
I AM not afraid!
My name is VICTORY!

Healing Virtue

In all things, the Bible reminds us that we are more than conquerors through Him who loved us. God tells us to fear not—for He is with us—and that He will help us and strengthen us. We must not forget that as long as we are born of God, we overcome the anxieties of the world and are victorious.

Remember: Your name is VICTORY!

Healing is a process.

Jessica Marie Schuuman
Edmonton, Alberta

Healing Affirmation

The present is the destination
where time touches ETERNITY.

Healing Virtue

Enjoying every moment of NOW
is the only important concept we as humans
need to be concerned about.

The Antidote

The greatest gift we are given is life.
So, enjoy every minute of your present.
Make yourself proud in each moment you take a breath.
Remember the past is gone and the future is not here yet.
How are you going to make an impact in your present NOW?

Healing Affirmation

"I am victorious because I am the righteousness of God,
and worthy of all good things."

Healing Virtue

We are more than conquerors through Him who loved us.
God tells us to fear not for He is with us and that
He will help us and strengthen us.
We must not forget that as long as we are born of God,
we overcome the anxieties of the world and are victorious.
Remember your name is VICTORY!

Twylia Reid

Healing Affirmation

"I can travel where my dreams take me,
and I can reach beyond what my eyes can't see."

Healing Virtue

The power of our words speaks volumes.
Death and life are in the power of the tongue!
Our perception of things matters, so we must be careful of the way we speak about how we perceive them to be.
Saying the words "I Can" brings out the power to refrain your thought-process from the undesirable to the desirable.

Twylia Reid

Healing Affirmation

"I am given beauty for ashes and endowed with
peace that surpasses all understanding."

Healing Virtue

We should not be anxious and worry about anything.
We must give God our ashes in exchange for His beauty.
God wants the wounded parts of our lives.
He will take care of those things that we need.
He already knows what they are; all we need to do is trust
Him and find rest in knowing that in return,
He will take care of us and all our cares.

Twylia Reid

Healing Affirmation

"Today I am unapologetically me."

Healing Virtue

We should not try to mold ourselves in knots trying to be like anyone else.
We must have the courage to be who God made us to be and live the life God called us to live. Others' expectations of me are unimportant and I will live in peace exactly as He created me to be!

Twylia Reid

Healing Affirmation

"I will walk by faith, not by sight.
I will walk, but never alone."

Healing Virtue

We should always be mindful to walk with God daily.
God wants walking partners.
The Bible says in Psalm 37:23 that
"*the steps of a good man are ordered by the Lord,
and He delights in his way*". When we walk with God,
our will is going to be aligned with
His will because we are walking side-by-side
with Him which keeps our focus on Him.

Twylia Reid

Wholeness
is your birthright.

HEALING THROUGH ME
Poet Annie Echevarria De Saquic
Rhode Island

A new day begins I open my eyes.

Still burning and blurry
For the tears I cried.
Is it possible?

Will I make it through?
Will my strength and my faith *today* be renewed?

As I press through the pain, a voice deep inside
sweetly and surely says,
"I'm by your side and
no burden too strong for you to bare
as long as you know that I AM here."

"Press through the pain
and you will see at the end of it all,
healing will be there.
"I am with you always
but you must see,
for you will help others
find healing through ME"

Tiesha Frontis
Durham, North Carolina

Healing Affirmation

I am cherished

Healing Virtue

I am protected and cared for through God's love for me.
This reminds me it is okay to love me enough to protect my heart and care for me on a daily basis. I learn to make self-love and self-care a priority in my life.

Ephesians 5:29
"For no one has ever hated his own body, but he nourishes and tenderly cares for it, as the Messiah does the church."

'Love' is an action word. You must make a commitment to yourself to take an active part in your healing process. It is so easy for us to want the best for others but now is the time for you to want the best for *you*.

So, you may say, *"How do I start wanting the best for me?"* Two ways are:

- Self-care by definition is any necessary human regulatory function which is under individual control, deliberate, and self-initiated.
- Self-love is regard for one's own well-being and happiness. In wanting the best for you, start to take time out of your schedule to listen to your heart when it is weary, listen to your mind when it is overwhelmed, and listen to your soul when it is troubled.

Cherish who you are. Embrace who you are becoming. Respect the process. Activate your love within you.

7 Daily Healing Affirmations for You

1. I value who I am and I value my self-worth.

2. I value my time and no longer will allow others to rob precious moments.

3. I love God and myself first and everything else will align.

4. I am love and I will love others in spite of their actions.

5. I am willing to sacrifice my time in order to get to know who I am and to love me.

6. I am worth the time it takes to allow the authentic me to be revealed.

7. I choose to be who God created me to be unapologetically.

THE HEALING PROCESS
Poet Joy Jallah
Monrovia, Liberia

God can sometime let His beloved go
through things in life that will allow the process of healing.

The healing occurs when God's beloved can go through pain
that can build their faith. It can strengthen them to not give up.

However, to focus more on faith.
To be strong and of a good cheer in the healing journey.
God sent His Word and heal thy. Everything God's beloved goes through,
it is truly to reveal the glory of God.

A heart that is broken can be fixed by God.
A lonely heart can be filled with joy and satisfied by God.
Sometimes, going through things in life can only be a test of faith.
It can bring the best out of God's beloved people.
God can restore lives.

Genae Kulah
Compton, California

Healing Affirmation

I am my sister's complement not competition.
We are all interconnected; I cannot be fully me without you.

Healing Virtue

Philippians 4:2-4
"I urge Euodia and I urge Syntyche to agree in the Lord. Yes, I also ask you, true partner, to help these women who have contended for the gospel at my side, along with Clement and the rest of my coworkers whose names are in the book of life. Rejoice in the Lord always. I will say it again: Rejoice!"

The comparison and competition game is real among women in the world. The sad thing is that it is also real with women in the church. When more than one woman is preaching, you can hear people state things like, "I like her" or "She was my favorite" or "She did not preach as well as..." And for those of us who are doing the preaching, we internally say, "I did not do that well", "I was off today", or "I wish I could preach like so and so". I cannot stand this! It makes me ask, "When did preaching become a contest between fellow workers in God?"

Paul dealt with a similar situation in *1 Corinthians 1:12-14.* What I am saying is this: Each of you says, "I'm with Paul" or "I'm with Apollos" or "I'm with Cephas" or "I'm with Christ." Is Christ divided? Was it Paul who was crucified for you? Or were you baptized in Paul's name?"
The answer to all those questions is NO. A 'no' then and a 'no' now.

As we look at the text, we see Paul urging Euodia and Syntych leaders in the church to agree in the Lord.

Paul was urging them to put aside their "differences or disputes" for the sake of the gospel. And the fact that Paul had another fellow believer to assist them suggests that it had a negative impact on the church. Because whether we want to admit it or not, we do impact the church when we are not working together toward the common goal of advancing God's kingdom and not our own.

When we choose to have an "I" infection—meaning we are focusing on ourselves and competing or comparing with one another—we:
- Cause division in the church. This is something God truly hates.
- Cause someone to turn away from the gospel.
- Tell God He made a mistake making us the way He made us.

It was no mistake that Paul chose to describe the church as the "Body of Christ". The parts of the body cannot operate on their own. Every part needs the other part to move the body in the direction the head tells it to go. As it is in the natural, so it is in the spiritual. The Head of the body is Jesus Christ and where He tells the body to go, we must go. But we cannot do that if we devalue one another by competing instead of complementing one another. Think of a woman or a few women who you can complement knowing that when our sisters are operating according to their God given abilities we, in turn, are blessed. No one can do what they do and no one can do what we do, but together we bring HARMONY.

I MIGHT BE HEALED
Poet Christina Wilson
Atlanta, Georgia

I was told it takes time.
That you have to be on a spiritual grind to reclaim
the time you had before tragedy.

The crazy thing about healing is that you don't even know you need it.
Most times, those obstacles don't look possible until defeated.
But you can always feel those tears fall.

Can feel that smoke in the back of your throats:
how I coped with it.
A bottle, sometimes stolen from my own father,
that's how I know it's back.
The sex and the shame; it's all one in the same when the
healing ain't done right.

In the words of Marvin Gaye: Sexual healing is a must.
I think that's why I feel best right after I make a man bust.
Cause nothing feels better than you being in control after a man takes
it upon himself to imagery his being into your very soul.

Figuratively and literally, I was broken more with every thrust which is
why now I tend to feel better after another cup.
A trick I learned from my daddy that when the going gets tough, just
take a shot to get past.

Take two shots when your heart breaks.
But he never gave me the number to take when your rapist is
heartless.
It's kinda hard to heal when the knife keeps cutting in the same spot.
In the words of Solange, I tried to drink it away.

I mean, I came a long way, but I think I went the wrong way.
I'm sorry. I wish this poem had a happy ending;
And I wish that I could say that after a few months go by, the healing is done and the pain disintegrates.

But sometimes you need to know that it's okay to take some time to get to that final stage of healing.

You may need someone to tell you it is okay for you to cry.
It's okay to wake up and not want to see the morning sky.

Because that's the part of healing they don't tell you that you need: The part about your heart feeling like it's been cursed with an everlasting bleed.

Healing is hard.

That's about as poetic as it gets.

Betty Speaks
Greenville, South Carolina

June 26, 1996, I was involved in a terrorist attack while on a military assignment in Saudi Arabia. The force of the explosion was extremely deadly over 300 hundred of us were wounded and 19 were killed. Throughout the search and rescue for survivors one couldn't help but contemplate on being the next to be killed.

Healing Affirmation

I am going to live.

Healing Virtue
Affirming that I shall live and not die,
the calling is not on my life just yet.
There is, indeed, a purpose for this surviving this life happening.
"My days are multiplied, and the years of my life are increased".
Proverbs 9:11

December 2012, I received surgery on my left eye because of flying debris that had damaged my retinae. The doctors indicated that I would never see the same again and that I could potentially go blind in this eye.

Healing Affirmation

I am not going blind.

Healing Virtue
Nothing is impossible for me to see if I remain FOCUSED,
have Faith, and follow through with my mission.

Years after retiring from the Army, I experienced having horrific headaches. The severe pain caused a throbbing sensation to the back of my neck and the crown of my head. The actual sounds of military vehicles and weapons were still vivid in my head. The sound of a back blast from a car didn't help, nor could I at that time tolerate sounds coming from trains, plains, or heavy-duty paraphernalia.

Healing Affirmation
I am not having headaches.

Healing Virtue
I can hear the beautiful sound, an inspiration of the birds humming melodies, and I am conscious of the here and now sounds that are clear and vivid—sounds that purposely block out the annoyance of those sounds that triggered headaches.

I dealt with a variety of transitional issues upon retiring from the military. For the most part, I had been experiencing a great deal of socialization skills with nonmilitary individuals. I felt as though I had entered an unfamiliar world. A world that was not orderly. A world that was filled with offensive behaviors and disrespectful attitudes by people who reminded me of irritating parasites. People who didn't take the time to appreciate a person who nearly lost her life for her country.

Healing Affirmation

I am no longer irritated.
I am rejuvenated with greatness and gratification.

Healing Virtue
Sometimes when God takes you into a blessing, your crowd gets smaller.

Bitterness is one of the uttermost controlling adversaries in the form of Christ currently. Honestly, do you know how many ailments or weaknesses are right related to bitterness?
I love knowing and educating the people named to labor in healing and deliverance should know when dealing with illnesses better to learn if the person standing or sitting before them has an issue with bitterness.

It is critical to learn if there are people that one have yet pardoned or forgiven. It is essential to request from the individual when in their lifetime where they identified with their sickness. It is important to ask the individual what life events were going on at or near that time. Frequently, the following are distinctive answers a person might give. I've encountered infidelity. I lost my husband as a result and the house which we purchased together. I could have let another person go because I was there longer. These are two of many reasons any person could share as to why they've not forgiven someone.
People have instantly been healed of their bitterness on the spot once this unforgiveness has been taken care of spiritually.

Healing Affirmation
I am healed from bitterness

Healing Virtue
Bitterness and anger towards those that caused pain to me willfully or intentionally wronged me will not prevail!
I am in control of my destiny and happiness.

Will thou be made whole?

GOD CAN RESTORE LIVES.
Poet Joy Jallah
Monrovia, Liberia

When life seems hopeless,
God can restore.

When life is not in alignment,
God can put things back in place.

God can restore the broken-hearted.
God can change things around all for His purpose and plan.

God can repair the mind that seems like giving up.
God can fix what seems like there is no way.

God can make a way out of no way.

God is a miracle-working
God who can restore damaged lives.

Brittany Peterson
St. Petersburg, Florida

Healing Affirmation

In Christ, I am complete and I have everything that I need.

I am chosen, celebrated, and cherished.

Healing Virtue Antidote

In search of acceptance and validation, I settled in situations that were conditional, detrimental, and left me empty. Choosing what was familiar made it difficult to set the standard for what would produce fruitfulness in my life. Though I struggled, my search for belonging ended when I learned that all along, the love I desired awaited me in the heart of Christ. I am healed by this truth: Christ is **all** that I need and through His love I know that I am accepted, valued, and complete.......and so are YOU! Beloved, your worth is not attached to anyone or anything. All that you are and everything that you need is found in Him.

"To know the love of Christ which passes knowledge; that you may be filled with all the fullness of God"
(Ephesians 3:19 NKJV).

ABOUT THE AUTHORS

 **Brittany Peterson** graduated from the University of Central Florida with a bachelor's degree in criminal justice. With a testimony of her own, Brittany devotes her time to advocating for children who have been abused. She enjoys the work she does and is committed to raising awareness about child abuse. As a certified youth life coach, Brittany is passionate about supporting girls through their struggles by helping them overcome obstacles while increasing their confidence during the process. Brittany is currently in graduate school to become a counselor and after graduation she plans to continue serving children who have experienced trauma.

Betty Speaks is the Executive Director at *Strap Em' Up Boot Camp* and the founder of *Betty Speaks "IT"*. She is a CLC that specializes in Intentional Transformation, and LIFE rehabilitation. Betty is an the Army Veteran, Ambassador to The Veteran Woman LLC., a Global Network Virtual Marketer and Entrepreneur, 4x Best Selling Author, Ordained Pastor, Jesus Woman at Godheads Ministry, Ambassador to the Pink Pulpit Crusade International, and a Designated Mastery Story Teller.

She holds a BS in Business Management from the University of Maryland. She received 5 Outstanding Businesswoman of The Year awards from the American Business Women's Association. Betty Speaks passion and life's calling is to help others not just survive, but thrive in the face of chances, changes or challenges.

My Dedication

I give honor to God for His presence in my life, and to the person who has my (6); my earthly and Kingdom battle buddy **Drill Sergeant Steven Sullivan**. *His favorite mantra is "I believe all of God's promises for my health and healing.*
Jeremiah 17:14"!

 **Genae *"The Destiny Designer"* Kulah** is an ordained prophetic minister, founder of The Word 4 H.E.R. (Healed, Empowered, and Restored) ministry, empowerment coach, and bestselling author. She has received her Bachelor of Science in Biblical Studies and Business Administration, as well as certification as a church and discipleship consultant. Pastor Kulah the Ambassador trainer for the Pink Pulpit Crusade International, under the direction of Apostle Dr. Marilyn Porter

Tiesha C. Frontis is the founder and CEO of Know Your Self Worth, Inc. This organization, birthed in 2013, was created to inspire, uplift and teach women how God sees them and how they should see themselves through Him. She is a native of Charlotte, NC but relocated to Durham, NC in 1993 to pursue her college education at North Carolina Central University where she graduated with a dual Bachelor Degree in Chemistry and Biology. She believes education is important and is currently pursuing a dual Master's Degree at Pfeiffer College and will also pursue her Doctorate in Theology. She wholeheartedly believes in her movement...Know Your Self-Worth. She is a woman of purpose, faith and virtue, having persevered through diverse challenges including molestation, promiscuity, addiction, domestic abuse, miscarriage, homelessness, divorce and so much more. She lives to share her story with other women and men, encouraging them that they can make it and they can survive. She is a true testimony of resilience and triumph.

 Jessica Schuuman

Editor of 3 Times #1 Bestselling book 'The Unstoppable Woman of Purpose.' Content writer, and Black Sheep Weirdo Visionary who seeks to unleash your meaning and God given purpose through God's word alone.

My Dedication

I dedicate this to my first born son, Jack. This is for everything you have done in mine and DADA's life, I could never repay you enough. A true miracle in disguise, you have allowed me to see the warrior within. I love you forever and eternity, your Mum; Jessica.

 **Rebecca Adams** is a mindset and breakthrough coach, co-author, life and business coach, network marketer and influencer. She has had businesses since 2003 and is focused on the VALUE she gives and IMPACT she creates in her work. Her highest ability is to see the positive in any negative situation and change people's MINDSET into more positive, productive thinking by motivating them to concentrate on their personal development and gratitude daily. Rebecca's love for her Faith in God is paramount to her life and journey. She is a Mum of 2 children, of which, her son has special needs.

www.rebeccaadamsbiz.com

 **Twylia Reid** is a native of Columbus, Mississippi who currently resides inSavannah, Georgia. She obtained a B.S. Degree in Business Management atTrident University International, and is a 20 year United States Army retiree.

She's a published author, speaker, group facilitator, minister, entrepreneur, and

Founder / creator of Broken Wings Brain Injury Empowerment Group. She's also a 2017 Indie Author Legacy Award Author of the Year finalist.

Passionate about her role as a brain injury advocate and caregiver, she was inspired to write her first book "Broken Wings", to encourage, uplift, and inspire others affected by the devastation brain injury causes.

My Dedication

First to My Lord and Savior Jesus Christ for giving me the courage to step out on faith and be a part of this amazing project. Then, to my husband, Dexter, God knew what He was doing when He brought us together. To my children, NaSharee Delese Davenport and Mylon RaShaun Flournoy, you two are truly the wind beneath my wings. Last, but certainly not least, my parents, Arthur and Vera Flournoy. Without you two there will be no me. The values you've taught me are ones that I carry with me everywhere I go.

Randie Forne has 40 plus years in the entertainment industry to his credit. As a singer, songwriter, actor, playwright and poet, Randie is truly an industry icon. Randie has sang back with Grammy Award winning Gospel artist such as Shirley Caesar and been the opening act for R&B great, R. Kelly. He is a staunch activist for community and social issues, such as; HIV/AIDS, Breast Cancer, homelessness and troubled youth.

He is the founder and creative director of R.F. Entertainment Productions – an organization committed to offering opportunities and building platforms for lower-class youths and adults of the community who have extraordinary creative aspirations.

Randie, is the mastermind behind the highly acclaimed stage hit, anti-gang theater production - "Bang No More" which continues to air on Time Warner Cable in Raleigh, NC.

 **Christina Danielle Wilson** is a millennial mogul in the making – an actress, bestselling author, spoken word artist and poet, and the CEO of The Chris Dannie™ Brand – she is making waves in the world at just 20 years old! She was born in Prince George's County Maryland raised *"everywhere –* a bona fide military brat, she considers Temple, GA (20 miles west of Atlanta) home. She is a theater major at GA State University – where is scheduled to graduate May 2019.

She has 2 spoken word CD compilations to her credit and can be seen on the FOX network hit show Star in the 2017 season.

 **Balkaran Signh** is a poet and writer, He enjoys writing from historical points of view.

 **Annie Echevarria De Saquic** is a housewife who lives in Providence Rhode Island with her husband Pedro, son Pedro Samuel and dog Tyson. She enjoys being a mentor and working part time with differently abled people.

 **Joy Jallah** is a poet and writer. She is a regular contributor to "Women's Frontline Magazine".

Hurt people,

Hurt people.

Get healed!

HEALING NOTES

HEALING NOTES

HEALING NOTES

About The Publisher

Scatter Brained Genius Media Group (SBG Media Group) is the brainchild of Dr. Marilyn "M.E" Porter – who is an International Bestselling Author and accomplished publisher. SBG Media began as *Soulidified Publishing* – which was simply created for the purpose of Dr. Porter branding her own books under the parent company (at the time) Pearly Gates Publishing LLC, owned by her dear friend and colleague Mrs. Angela Edwards.

Soulidfied become SBG Media Group in 2017 when Dr. Porter brought the publishing house under the umbrella of her new company SBG Enterprises – which is a one stop shop for her clients.

To date SBG Media has produced 6 bestselling authors and 10 Amazon Bestsellers, to include 2 international.

SBG Media is a faith-based publisher and does not engaged in publishing; pornographic, occultism, racist, or otherwise derogatory material or anything that denounces Jesus Christ as Savior.

Are you looking for an author opportunity?

AFFIRMATIONS AND ANTIDOTES
THAT STRENGTHEN ME
BOOK #3 IN THE SERIES

1000 WORDS
100 WORD BIO
EDIT AND PROOFREAD
PROFESSIONAL FORMAT
VIRTUAL LAUNCH EVENT
1 PROMO MEME

investement required

THESCATTERBRAINEDGENIUS@GMAIL.COM

Visit –

www.thescatterbrainedgenius.com/publishing

to find more opportunities

www.ingramcontent.com/pod-product-compliance
Lightning Source LLC
Chambersburg PA
CBHW070552300426
44113CB00011B/1877